TRAPPED IN COMFORT ZONE

Compiled by:
Zarlish Waheed

First Edition Published in 2022 by
Brown Page Publication
29(a) Faizupur Khadar, Tigaon 90
Ballabgarh, Faridabad, Haryana, India (121101)
Whatsapp: 7428778978

Prologue

This book is all about comfort zones. All of us are somehow trapped in their comfort zone, we are trying to leave that zone or trying to stay in that zone. According to psychology ;

A comfort zone is a psychological state in which things feel familiar to a person and they are at ease and in control of their environment, experiencing low levels of anxiety and stress.

Some will say a comfort zone is bad as it will make you complacent and you won't learn new skills while some will say that being in a comfort zone will make you confident and reduce anxiety. Both might be right but we are not here to pass a judgmental statement. This anthology comprises twelve authors around the globe with their different experience and different thoughts yet united under the same theme. Every writer is unique in itself and their different views on comfort zones. This anthology is a combination of prose, poetry, sci-fi and short stories. And we are presenting their sentiments in front of you in the form of a book that you are holding in your hands. This book is unique in the way that all the thoughts and emotions of co-authors are penned down in a very alluring manner.

Little message for readers;

" The only important thing in the book is the meaning that it has for you".

~W. Somerset Maughamome.

Acknowledgement

This book is dedicated to my father "**MIAN ABDUL WAHEED**" for supporting me in every single decision I took and for making my dreams come true. Then I would like to thank Brown Page Publication for giving me this beautiful opportunity. Huge thanks to all the co-authors for putting trust in my words and letting me compile their precious work in my anthology. I would like to thank my family specially Mama, Abdul Malik, Zarnab and others as it wouldn't be possible without their support. Their encouragement has led me to the path of success. I am truly grateful for having them beside me. Thanks a bunch to Uncle Dr. Badar-e-Alam, Mian Irfan Fyyaz, Auntie Dr. Memona Majida, Nana abu Captain Abdul Basit, Mian Badar Munir, Uncle Mian Shabir Ahmed, Uncle Mansoor Khalid Akhtar, Uncle Ch. Amjad Ali. I would like to thank my friends (Habiba ashfaq, Sana Asif, Anusha Farooqi, Iqra Rafique Maida Iftikhar, Isha Ijaz, Eiman and other gems) that supported me at every step while compiling of this anthology. Very special thanks to auntie Ansa Ghazanfar for her criticism that always motivated me to do more! Thanks to my teachers because of them I'm at this point today.

Index

FOUNDER

Piyush Arora.

Piyush Arora was born on 26th May 1996 in Faridabad, Haryana.He completed his schooling in Haryana only in 2014 and started his preparations for Chartered Accountant but his dream is attracting him to become a writer. He wrote his debut novel in 2015 My Childhood Love with becomeshakespeare.com, Mumbai. After that, he never stopped himself to walk on the pathway to become a writer. Life of war is his second novel published in 2017 with Ranbir Singh under Notion Press, Chennai. Passion about Love 2018 Published on Kindle, eBook, and paperback available in both formats. He is also a part of more than 140 anthologies since 2020. Brown Page Publication is dedicated to his father . Piyush is doing very hard work to achieve this dream for his Father.

Rising Poetry Star, Poetic Group founded by Piyush in 2018 Pan India Poetry group for the writers where he usually upload voice notes or videos of poets every week on their YouTube channel but for now it's a part of its publication.Rising Poetry Star organizes an open mic session every Sunday over Google meet.

Contact:
Email: riskys1179@gmail.com
Instagram: poet.Piyush & yqbhaiya

THE COMFORT ZONEIS A TRAP.

Comfort zone is a trap, I can say because I usually felt the same. I am Piyush Arora, an ordinary boy from Faridabad, Haryana. I love my dream of writing. It became my passion when I passed 12th standard and I read the novel "Half Girlfriend". The book was given as present by Mr. Chetan Bhagat when I visited World of Wonder(WoW), a mall in Noida.

After reading the novel I planned everything to write my first novel "My Childhood Love" in 2015 that time I was just 18 years old. While writing the novel I learnt a big lesson of my life that If I want to complete the novel I have to sacrifice all those things which were using me to spend their time. Like, Facebook, Instagram, or other social media things. I have a Personal computer on that day but I can't keep myself busy on the computer because I am preparing for C.A these days. So I kept myself out of my comfort zone and started writing my first novel on my smartphone.

When I started writing I found another problem, which is time. 60% of my day is kept busy in my studies, 20% in traveling from home to institute & institute to home. Again I came out of my comfort zone. I make myself comfortable in a discomfort zone while traveling in public vehicles. I usually found a place where I could stand or sit without any disturbance while people bored the vehicle or debored it.

I am scared these days to talk with strangers and I have to find the publisher now to publish my book because in just one month my whole story was completely typed in my phone in a word file which is ready to publish.
I searched for the details for publishers to self publish my book, I got a call from a publisher located in Bombay. I completely got the knowledge to self publish the book after the call, but the problem I am facing now is trust just through a random call. How can I pay such a huge amount for self-publishing my book? I came out of my comfort zone again. I used to talk with my dad. Firstly he refused to publish such a book, Later on I convinced him & Visited to Bombay to meet the publisher after the meeting I got convinced to publish my book with them.

Moral of the Story:

When you can convince yourself than you can convince any person in the world, If you wants to came out from the comfort zone make your mind set ready once it has been done than no body can make you uncomfortable in my zone, no task will make you discomfort in your mind, just focus on the goal, but don`t make yourself habitual of any zone sometime take the rest is always necessary.

Coming out of your comfort zone is the first step towards success.

Editor & Co Author

<u>Navdeep kaur</u>

Navdeep kaur was born on 26th may 1998 in shahkot ,punjab.she loves to write since the age of twelve years.she started writing with the four liner and then writing became her passion.she use to write for her friends.Bt her first step towards her dreams that she taken by her first anthology that is (never give up).she is also doing theater since the days of college and win national level competition in plays,mimms and nukkad nataks.she has great leadership qualities that's why she represent her school and college at national level competitions and win also. She completed her graduation last year .After that she started working on her dream to be an Author as well as Anker .She participated in more than 60 + anthologies.she participated in many open mics and won the titles . Right now she is working as a community head of Rising poetry stars and Editor Of Brown page publication and recently she started compiling also.

Email:navdeepkaurnavi959@gmail.com

TRAP

Sometimes we are all trapped in our own thoughts. maybeIt's our own insecurities or we can say that our mind works like it. We make our own stories. But somehow we know that it's a harsh reality of our inner voice.we ignore it. We refuse to listen to it but it's time to listen to our own voice to confront what's the issue between you and your inner voice.

Today I am sharing a short story with you guys about a little Girl . Who has the guts to listen to herself.

A little girl.who loves to question about everything.who have a curious mind.But one answers her that makes her short tempered. time flies now that little girl is now a teenager and we all know this age is full mysteries we develop multiple talents,emotions & fears ,That what happens to her.when ever she ask questions everyone laughs at her .Whenever she wants to do something different everybody call her weird.when ever She achieve something everyone left her alone.When ever she do something for someone they always backstab her.That affects her a lot and suddenly She started do nothing .She never ask anything.A little fairy who love to fly. Now I feel trapped. Her little dreams are now broken.Bt the worst thing that happens to her.She easily accepted that she is weird that's why everyone left her alone.She doesn't have any friend circle or even a single best friend who can support her. Now she started feeling comfortable in this situation and that's the time when she trapped in her fake comfort zone.Its not her,it's her mind who makes her work and think like this .Bt as we all know change is constant Finally a person who understand her.who have answers of her questions.who can solve her all mysteries Arrives and it's her new teacher.They both share a different kind of connection I think this is the reason they can communicate better.teacher talked to her every day and now she start breaking every chain that makes her trapped.She break her silence and now she became who really she is.teacher make her write every day whatever she feel and also give her direction towards some creative line and in result that little girl became a poetess .Now she talks through her pen.

PROJECT HEAD.

Sonia Paruthi is a young blooming writer in the field of literature who began the journey at the age of sweet sixteen and brought laurels for her work. She belongs to a beautiful place renowned as land of Gods and Goddesses i.e. Uttarakhand. She started the voyage at the allpoetry.com where she won 35 gold,33 silver,28 bronze and 73 honorable mention. Moreover 23 pieces of her work had been on the front page of the web. She has also won the honorable mention in The All India Essay Writing Event organized by Shri Ram Chandra Mission in collaboration with the United Nations Information Centre for India and Bhutan & Heartfulness Education Trust on the theme "There is a wisdom of heart and a wisdom of head". She has a good leadership quality which is evident from the captainship granted to her at the school level to represent the school. She belongs to the Science background and has knowledge about core Java. She has participated in many anthologies and written for many websites. She has published books titled Daastan-e-zindagi, Do dil ek jaan, safar _e_jazbaat , You feel right? under Brown Page Publication where she is working as Training Head, Project Head and a compiler as well. Her work leaves a lasting impression on readers' hearts, minds and souls.

Contact:

Email: soniaparuthipsychology@gmail.com

Instagram : feel_in_poetry

COMPILER

Zarlish Waheed.

Zarlish Waheed is an 18 years old writer. She belongs to "Khori Alam" from Punjab, Pakistan. She started writing back in 2016 as a hobby. She did her matriculation from Wisdom House Channan and her Intermediate in pre-medical from Punjab Group Of Colleges. Then her interest in chemistry led her to study BS Chemistry from University Of Gujrat.

Her hobbies include painting, reading, writing, drawing, learning new skills and languages. She can speak English, Urdu, Punjabi and German. Her writings mostly include prose but sometimes she tries poetry as well. Her career plan includes being a research scientist. She is the eldest among her siblings. She is very ambitious and always eager to learn new things.

Contact: Instagram: @trapped_in_my_mind47

Email; zarwaheed47@gmail.com

ZARLISH WAHEED

I wonder what would transpire if we resided outside our comfort zone. Would that ineluctably make discomfort comfortable?

Would we run alongside the challenges we once veered away from? Perhaps it'd make our encephalon swell up from all the sagacity acquired and our souls in a constant state of revisioning.

Change only feels uncomfortable when it's first introducing itself, like an incipient menu that hasn't quite earned our trust yet. But once we grow fond of the tickling monarch wings of an incipient tomorrow, we seldom wish ourselves back to yesterday. The artifice is making the initial leap despite not kenning where we'll land. So many of us become trapped in the quicksand of comfort because we forget how expeditiously we acclimatize to incipient environments. We forget that Where we're headed is most often better than what we're leaving behind. If we were betokened to stay planted in minuscule flower pots without room to stretch our roots, there would be no point to our being.

We'd be subsisting, but we wouldn't be living. We'd be racing one another to mediocrity and stunted magnification.

If we were designated to stay planted in diminutive flower pots without room to stretch our roots, there would be no

Point to our being. We'd be subsisting, but we wouldn't be living. We'd be racing one another to mediocrity and stunted magnification. Someone once told me that comfort is the most detrimental thing to the adventurous spirit. I believe that comfort aliments on those most susceptible to reluctance. Those who become hesitant around incipient settings, companionships, habits, traditions, or worldviews are closing themselves off to a plethora of incipient possibilities, a decision that is often propelled by fear.

Sometimes progression denotes landing in poison ivy rather than a field of wildflowers. Sometimes it denotes getting hurt before we can make it to where we're designated to thrive. But that's okay because we still got our feet off the ground. And sometimes even an erroneous turn can lead to a step in the right direction. And that single step can lead you toward an incipient perspective or an incipient perspective.

Maybe your unanswered prayer is God's way of

preserving you. Maybe the things you ached for were not genuinely going to give you any placidity or pleasure or comfort. Maybe all the things that broke you genuinely built you up to believe that your heart can sometimes apostatize you and your orchestrations sometimes fail you and that's okay. It's okay to opt for something so desperately only to realize it wasn't good for you. It's okay to admit that the things you fought for didn't fight as ruthlessly for you because maybe this is God's way of edifying you how to trust him, that if you let go, if you confide in his timing, if you don't endeavor so hard to rush things all the time, they will ineluctably fall into place.

May be the people you get affixed to when you know they're erroneous for you are just edifying you the paramountcy of letting go, of detaching from something you optate so much so you can find something preponderant. May be they're edifying you that temptations are not always gratifying, that some temptations look good from afar but leave you feeling empty when you get too proximate.

May be your heart moved for the erroneous people so you can find your way back to God or back to yourself. May be God wants your peregrination to be about yourself for now not about love and that's why he wants your heart to belong to you or he's edifying you how to be patient with your heart until it finds what it authentically deserves.
May be everything is working out the way it should

be and God's endeavoring to edify you to stop holding on so tightly to the resplendent picture in your head of how things are supposed to be and trust him to paint a marvelous picture instead. Trust him to turn the picture inside your head into a masterpiece.

Living life can be very challenging at times. Getting the hang of what works for you and what doesn't may take a very long time. Sometimes you get confused and frustrated by what you're doing, or where you're going.

You may try to follow your own wisdom, but there are times when your internal navigational systems may throw you way off course. You may be lured away from where you need to be. Often, this siren's call comes in the form of well-intentioned people who may want to help you direct your life so that you do "the right thing" But people are not always so well-intentioned.

Sometimes, we trust other people more than ourselves, accepting another's opinions and views as more valid than our own. Somehow, we think they know what's better for us than we do-or we've been told that so often that we come to believe it. It's frequently the early influence of our family that sets this scenario in motion. Sometimes, confusion about who we are and what is best for us involves a deep-seated conflict focusing on allegiances to and boundaries with people who we deemed vitally important to our lives. Unchecked, this same familiar pattern may find its way into future relationships with spouses, bosses, mentors, or friends.

For some people, it's just simpler to allow others to keep doing for them what they need to learn to do for themselves. For others, there is a naive expectation that things will just come their way without having to take action on their own to make it happen. Still other times, there may be an unspoken agreement to sacrifice one's own authenticity in return for Love.

The bottom line is that by not taking responsibility for ourselves, we too often allow others to take responsibility for us. And in doing this we are essentially giving them permission to take charge of our lives. There is an enormous price to pay for giving your life away in this way.

It's simply not your life any longer; rather, it's someone else's projection of what your life should be.

To be able to open the heart again after apostasy, injury, or loss is a precious act. It requires both valance and commission. It requires an incipient movement to emerge from the depths of grief.

Forgiveness is one of the most certain paths to instauration, and it is additionally one of the most arduous.

However, it is an endeavor to return to wholeness, once again, by letting go and liberating myself from the tight clutch and cumbersomely hefty encumbrance of caution, vexation, resentment, and the desire for revenge and penalization. In forgiving others, I free myself towards belonging and wholeness, be it with the person I am forgiving, or with myself.

Stop worrying about other people understanding you. Get in touch with yourself instead. Fixate on what makes you jubilant, what makes your soul feel at placidity, you are your most sizably voluminous commitment,

So start doting your imperfections, your inelegance, your weirdness, your intensity, your susceptibility, your everything. Life becomes so much more consummating when you are just simply yourself. The world keeps spinning whether people understand you or not so why not make this next trip around the sun about you.

Most of us are never authentically present in the moment because we are perpetually making plans about the future, cogitating the past, being apprehensive about what's to come or feeling culpability and vaingloriousness of what has been. Our society is built up in a way that perpetually makes our focus shift from present to past & future.So is it even possible to be present in the moment while going through our quotidian lives?

There are perpetually decisions to be made, plans to decipher, meetings to go to... But if we bring cognizance to everything we do, we still can be present even in the midst of everything. We do not become present by perpetually celebrating "I require to be present", but by shifting the perspective from being the ruminator to being the visual examiner of the celebrations. The moment you describe that you are not present, you are.

"I hope you find acceptance. The kind that rings through your bones, the kind that mutes the voice inside of you that tells you that you are not adequate, or that you are falling behind. I hope you forgive yourself for the mistakes you have made, for the past you sustain inside of you. I hope you learn to let go - of the things you had to do in order to rejuvenate, or to grow, or to survive. You are doing your best. You are human. Please don't ever forget that. I hope you find the kind of moments that take your breath away. The kind of moments that transmute you. I hope you peregrinate to places that cleanse you, I hope you go to concerts that ring through your bones and make you feel alive. I hope you surround yourself with the kinds of friends that embolden your spontaneity, that are always there for you. I hope you live. Genuinely. I hope you don't abstain. There is so much to feel in this world. I hope you feel it all.But most of all, I hope you find yourself out there. I hope you decipher your heart, I hope you decipher your mind. I hope you learn how to be kind to yourself, how to embrace the peregrination you are on. I hope you learn how to be proud of the person you are becoming, I hope you learn how to be proud of where you are even if it isn't precisely where you optate to be.I hope you learn to fall in love with the process, with the messiness of life and the mystification of it all". ♥

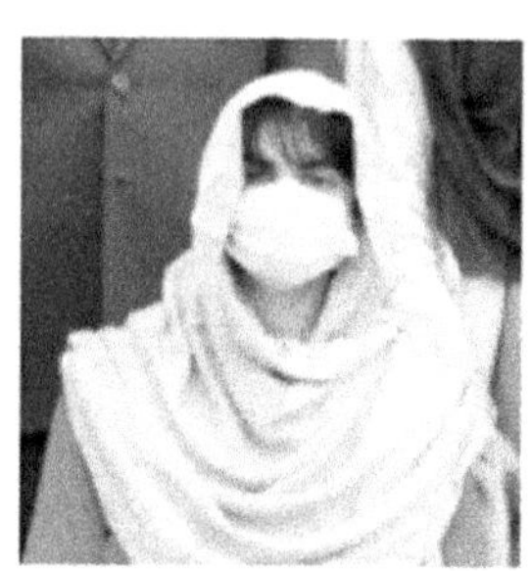

Ayesha Areej Akhtar

I'm Ayesha from Pakistan. An M.Phil. I am an English Literature student. Art is my love, be it poetry, prose, music or painting. My poems are little sanctuaries for all the emotions too overwhelming for my heart. So Dive in! You can also find me ranting in rhythms on

Instagram: @spyrrhicia

TITLE: COLD-BLOODED WARMTH.

My hands reach out constantly,
For anyone in need of an embrace,
Yet the touch of another body,
Is categorized by my mind as a foreign object,
And my heart begins to freeze.
My warm limbs are infested with frozen veins,
That turn into fatal tendrils at the
slightest threat of invasion,
By the orange glow of cracking woods in
the fireplace of an abandoned temple.
For me;
The sight of wild winds extinguishing life,
And the remaining clues of existence embodied
by the smoke coughed out by a broken chimney,
Is delightful.
So these eyes of mines that cry tears of sympathy,
Are they mere consequences of my
defense mechanisms?
To convince myself of my empathy,
Do I burn fires in abandoned temples in the
middle of scorching sand storms?
That my desire infected brain
disguises as snow storms?
Do I burn myself to be free of my own cold blood?

Or is my cold blood the cure to this
fire that engulfs me?

TITLE: TRAPPED IN A COMFORT ZONE.

I cannot breathe,
These walls keep closing in,
Suffocation grips my lungs,My
heart threatens to stop,
I scream!Silently. Because,
This 3 by 4 feet prison cell,
Is the only place I can call home.
I live in a dystopia within a dystopia,
But at least I know the limits of the former,
I have long befriended its demons,
And its thorns and shackles have
now become my jewels.
The human sized mirrors on these walls,
Reflect my fears,From every angle,
In every inch of my being,They remind me,
How my legs had burned,
When I took a mere step out
into,That vicious freedom.
How I had to writhe in pain,
And what will become of me,
When the monsters out there devour me.
So,
I will let these maggots eat my flesh,
Slowly rot to death,
In these safe margins,Of my comfort zone.

TITLE: ONE OF THE SINNERS.

I have been a sinner for as long as I can remember,
A person who should have been executed long ago,
There is no disgusting deed that
I have not committed,
So I deserve all the retribution I get.
The lanes to my past are littered
with poisonous bushes,
Yet I frequently trace my way back and forth,
Again and again,
everyday,
And now my feet have swollen to the point of
decomposition.
But I will not stop.
Because this is my punishment.
I have been wondering,
Was this chance I begged for really what I wanted?
Because it's suffocating;
To despise myself and be happy.
I can't do this anymore,
So I will smudge myself with the blood I spilt,
Burn myself just enough to know what it feels like,
To know what pain is.
And then,
I will wait,

For this all to end,
Because in this life,
I was destined,
to be one of the sinners.

TITLE: RAINBOW AND LIGHTENING.

Those colors hung in midair,
their backs arched,
One on top of the other,
supported by invisible ropes,
That choked them.
When a blinding crack appeared in the sky,
Like a withered tree letting out its
last agonized breath,
A final effort to be known,
I realized what life truly is;
A beautiful wound,
the pain of which is the only thing
that keeps you going.

TITLE: INEVITABILITY OF DEATH:

Kindle the candle and leave it to melt,
Till these shadows halt.
This luminescence will eventually dim down,
Till it turns dark.

Sachin Jain

Sachin Jain is a Result Partner, TEDx Speaker, published Author & Director, MyLakshay Consulting. Behind this startup are 2 decades of practically living a Happy and Fulfilled life while enjoying every moment to serve and contribute to others.

He started his professional career with Bosch, a leading global automotive brand, as a Trainee in 1998 and reached the Key Account Manager position, before taking the voluntary exit in Feb 2020 and starting his venture. He was heading Institutional Sales and Customers management in the Northern region.

As a Result Partner, his vision is to help people and work along with them to come out of their comfort zone and bring the necessary clarity towards meaningful goals. They can achieve this by getting more aware and overcoming their limiting beliefs and accomplishing results driven by their values and needs. He believes that everyone can live a happy and fulfilled life when satisfying results are achieved on both personal and professional front while contributing to others' lives.

He has an MBA in International Business, OE Qualification from IIM, Bangalore customized executive program, Business Strategies for Emerging Markets from HSE University, and ICF

Certified Executive Coach from ILA.

Sachin has authored books "101 Empowering Golden Nuggets"," Decade Planner" and "How to Grow your Peanuts". Further, he has also Co-authored a Book "Champions of Change: True Stories of Transformation".

Know more about in digital space:-
Website: www.mylakshay.com
Award: https://www.iafindia.com/mr-sachin-jain/

GET COMFORTABLE BEING UNCOMFORTABLE

"A ship is always safe at the shore, but that is not what it is built for"- Albert Einstein

It was a Monday morning in March 2008, I was busy planning the task for the day. My phone buzzed unexpectedly as I don't get calls at this time in early business hours. The call was from my Departmental Head Mr. Harvinder.

"Sachin, how are you? We are just seeing the report you sent yesterday evening for last year's business. Once again our business from North is not up to the expectation and has not even crossed previous year's performance." He sounded upset.

"Good morning, yes, I know". While talking with him I was parallelly thinking of the reasons to justify the fall in the business.

He continued *"We have seriously accessed the continuity plan for our regional office in Agra. We have discussed internally, and it has been decided to close the local office."*

After hearing these words, I was feeling terrible inside and all the worst scenarios came up in my mind once the office was closed. I might lose my job and must start searching for a new job in Agra itself as I was comfortably settled and did not want to move out of my hometown.

"What are the options available apart from closing the office," I asked.

He continued *"We don't have an option for office and only look for an alternate location for handling the business operations. You need to decide on your transfer to the new location."*

"What is the new location," I asked him curiously.

He continued *"You have two options for a new location either you can choose Delhi or Chandigarh".*

"Sure, let me think and get back to you on this" I ended the conversation hastily as I was not feeling comfortable.

Now let me tell you the background of this conversation. I started my professional journey in May 1998 at the regional office of an automotive corporation in Agra, my hometown. As I got married in July 2002 and was blessed with a baby boy in August 2005.

I was responsible for the Punjab area along with my regional head who was representing Sales in the North region.

As I was comfortably staying in a joint family along with my grandparents and drawing a good salary with no major hiccups, I started feeling complacent and due to this reason, I was not interested in moving out of Agra for the job and wanted to comfortably continue what has become a routine now.

Only due to this during these 10 years, my first promotion was awarded in 2007 after 6 years of getting confirmed against every 3 – 4 years generally. I came across many better job opportunities, not only internal but also external, however I did not show any proactive approach towards them. Even during one of the yearly employee reviews, I even denied moving to other locations for a better position.

Subconsciously I was aware that I was not able to qualify for the promotion, rather could not even discuss the low increments in a few yearly salary reviews.

I even felt upset sometimes as my promotion was getting delayed due to being in this comfortable situation as I was more fearful of failures and challenges in taking up the new responsibility being offered.

As the business in the region was deteriorating year on year, continuing the stand-alone regional office was not economically viable for the corporate office to continue operation. Management has patiently waited for a continuous 3 business cycles before taking the call of discontinuing the office.

You might have encountered a similar situation or surprise in our lives, where we are stuck with surprise. Moreover, we don't have any solution which can be offered or any leniency available to continue the comfortable situation. The situation can be even worse than this, like in the first week of December

2021, the CEO of a startup in the US called up an online meeting and declared employment termination of its Employees just to compensate for the downside of the business call. Since this online meeting went viral, I have included it in this story. This was one of the instances of being surprised unexpectedly.

Friends, to come up from this situation I went into many rounds of discussions with my mentor and many hours of introspection and self-realization t6o find an appropriate answer.

It's a fact when you come across a defining moment in life you start thinking beyond your normal capacity. One important thing which I noticed was that I was not growing professionally and was missing participating in various events which were dreams for me.

When I started thinking about what I needed to do to achieve my dreams I was able to visualize the imaginary road to follow. I was able to understand what was wrong and I realized being too comfortable was bad for growth in my career.

This moment made me think in the direction of a growth mindset. It was something that made me feel confident and I chose Chandigarh and my success story went multifold from this moment ahead.

As expected, once I started taking newer roles and initiatives, I started attracting what was once a dream. I got my next promotion in 2011 and started attracting various accolades along with participation in various national and international events.

Let's understand briefly what went wrong, what do you mean by trapped in the comfort zone, and how to come out freely.

We feel safe when we are in a zone which we know and feel stress-free. The growth in this zone is limited to the knowledge we apply. When we are in our comfort zone, we limit ourselves and don't take a risk to get into stress. When we are having a list of pending tasks our minds will always opt for the least stressful task.

Subconsciously we tend to do maintenance tasks instead of productive tasks. Maintenance tasks are repetitive tasks that may not develop your career or life. Productive tasks are critical tasks that need to be completed and which impact your career and lead to growth in your life.

We need to understand our life priorities and the meaningful goals we need to achieve in our lives. We all have an aspiration to be successful in our lives. The definition of success is different for each one of us. It can be materialistic, money, wealth, relationship however the bottom understanding is you are expecting to reach a position far better than what you are into. It's like following the standard operating procedure. If you follow a routine you will receive the same results.

Let me share with you how I was able to get out of my comfort zone

-        Find a compelling reason to "*why I am doing what I am doing*"
-        Face the fear of uncertainty as it is only an

assumption.

-        Don't be overwhelmed, break the bigger task into smaller but meaningful steps.

-        Learn new knowledge in the direction of your goals.

-        Act.

The moral of my story is *"To grow in our lives we need to become comfortable in being uncomfortable"*.

Sharlet Mary Alvares.

Sharlet is a native of Goa and writing is what she does best. She is an English teacher in a reputed school in Mumbai and an online English tutor where she trains students all across the world in creative writing and public speaking. She composes songs, is a poet, teacher, singer and a creative writer.

Trapped in the comfort zone? Maybe you are on the right track. Getting trapped in your comfort zone is not all that bad. Why? I understand this means doing the things that are easy and being safe all the time. At times, people feel that we won't learn anything new if we don't take the calculated risks. Surprisingly, I'm here to express a different point. The famous scientist, Albert Einstein, was trapped in his comfort zone, according to me, where he only processed the length and breadth of physics. He was so much in love with this subject that it didn't take him much time to master it. He never stepped out of his comfort zone and learnt another subject or topic which did not interest him. At the end, he still achieved greatness and is forever remembered as a genius where you see it doesn't make a difference if you are trapped in your comfort zone because maybe that is where you belong. Maybe your goal is to perfect the field that you are already in and that will take you a long way in the future. Michelangelo was a popular Italian painter, sculptor, poet and engineer. He is remembered for his flawless work of art and even he was trapped in his comfort zone. He did what he was best at and that was art. No other artist was as popular as he was in his century. He transformed his comfort zone into a work of art which was appreciated by all. His famous sculptures of Peta and David are the epitome of perfection. It hardly mattered if he had enough confidence because at the end of the day only his work spoke for himself. It didn't matter if he was a great public speaker or if he was an articulate spokesperson because when people viewed his work, they understood that he had a great mind of a genius. Then out of all those who felt extremely challenged, we have Ludwig van Beethoven. He was passionate about music and even when his very own nature didn't support him, he did not give up. He started feeling the symptoms of deafness and realized that days would get tougher for him. There was a point where he also considered committing suicide but something stopped him from doing this terrible act of self-destruction. Instead, he chose to remain in his comfort zone and to ace it with the highest level of creativity. It is believed that the music songs he composed after getting deaf, were the most touching and outstanding pieces of art. In this case, how would you understand such challenges that come in life? As a blessing or a curse? I would vote for blessing because being deaf is what helped him to rise beyond the normal circumstances in life. Sir Issac Newton too, who is recognized as the father of science, hated his foster father but embraced the logic of science. Legend has it that as a young Issac Newton, he was sitting under an apple tree when he was bonked on the head by a falling piece of fruit. This is a common experience for many but what was special about Sir Issac is that by being in his comfort zone, he simply asked the question of 'Why.' This led him to discover and suddenly come up with his law of gravity. To achieve greatness, one shouldn't simply be different and creative but one should be meaningfully different and innovative. The Welsh actor, who won an Academy Award for best actor for his role as Hannibal Lecter in 'The Silence of the Lambs' who is Sir Anthony Hopkins, has also followed his heart. He is a renowned actor, director, producer, composer and painter who has left a mark on his audience in the field of art. No number of hurdles in his life could halt his growth because getting into the character came easy to him. This means he was always in his comfort zone no matter what role he was asked to depict in his movies. How beautiful is this type of comfort zone which only helps you to get into that trans of creativity!! Susan Boyle, a middle-aged church volunteer from a small town in Scotland, auditioned for Britain's Got Talent and won hearts all over the world. Her soaring vocals and humble personality caught the eyes of the beholders. She has released seven albums and even performed for the Queen. All she did was sing her favorite songs as comfortably as ever where they have skyrocketed to the Billboard charts. I have cited the examples of these famous figures because they rose against the criticism around them to gain the impossible. Everyone around you will tell you in which areas you need to be better and which areas you still have to work on but what I want you to have is a strong faith in yourself that you were made to achieve greatness and in this life itself you will nail your goal. Whenever you speak, speak by knowing that you can be stronger, you can be confident and you can be a good person no matter what situation arises in your life. Einstein, Michelangelo, Ludwig van Beethoven, Sir Isaac Newton, Sir Anthony Hopkins and Susan Boyle were also people like us and we can also become great individuals like them. There are many times we fail to understand our worth because of the comments we receive from people around us. The truth is, the law of nature is that nobody in this world can determine our level for us and we cannot judge the level for others. The universe is our ultimate judge. It knows where we have originated and where our calling will take us. We don't have to prove to anyone because each of us already have the God-given dignity and respect. When the chains of your comfort zone lock you down, where you feel trapped, then the best that you can do is melt them down and turn them into decorative ornaments. Confidence must not suppress the others, but build others to fly high into the wind. Come wind or storm, life must go on. Comfort zone is only a state of mind. The moment you believe you are an achiever, you will succeed. Failure in life is not bad, till you fail with dignity and learn life lessons from it. Today's failure can be the stepping stone of tomorrow's success. Broaden your horizon and deepen your knowledge, because you are still left with a lot of exciting experiences still to enter into your fruitful life. If you fail at 18, you can still complete your graduation at 22. If you don't get a job at 22, you can still become a teacher at 25. If you don't earn well at 25, you can still get married at 30 and have your own business. If you don't get married at 30, you can still adopt at 35 and save a life. If you don't have a family at 35, you can still become a famous actor and win an Oscar. It's never too late to earn achievements because we still have our whole life to show our talents. The useful qualities and traits that one can develop to master your comfort zone, can be as follows: 1. Get inspired – From inspiration, a masterpiece can be born. 2. Openness to experience – Be positive and be open to new experiences. Even if you become a victim of a negative experience, don't let them hurt you. These experiences always direct you towards your goal. They are only guiding you. 3. Critical thinking – Never study only what is assigned to you or what will only help you to fetch a certificate. Always research more and learn more. 4. Precision – Always work with precision. It can be the smallest work of art, but it still has to be organized and authentic. It still can be made perfect. All in all, do not forget to flow in your creativity and enjoy the ride because if you get bored, then the audience will get bored too. Always say yes to new opportunities and always give your hundred percent no matter how small a task it is. At the end, it is not how much we do, but how much love we put into doing these things when trapped in our comfort zone. Believe, Be Brave, Become the one that you wish to be.

Dr. Vikas Kumar Singh.

Dr Vikas Kumar Singh is an international marketing strategist and author of his first book "Return Ticket " . Vikas has spent over 2 decades in the corporate sector and has rich experience of international markets . Dr Singh holds Doctorate in Philosophy(PhD) from Lucknow university and has interest towards ancient Greek Philosophy which has now become his passion & area of study. Vikas aspires to impact maximum people in this world so that they can realize their true potential and excel in their chosen profession .He believes in having a student mindset and wisdom of life long learning . He is always open to learning new subjects and concepts !

As our island of knowledge grows, so does the shore of our ignorance. ---------- John Archibald Wheeler

Have you ever felt that you are stuck in a hamster wheel? So, to keep sync with the fast changing world , although you are running faster in your personal and professional life , you are doing your best by working for more hours, you are changing all your personal priorities & family responsibilities before the professional work but at the end of the day you find that the results are not changing at all . Your boss still remains unhappy and angry . You hate your job but still toil everyday due to fear of losing it .Well , let me say without doubt that you are trapped in a comfort zone . I have found that most of the people that are stuck in this situation are always in denial mode .They tell stories of misfortune & fate. They blame it on external circumstances and bad luck . They explain that lady luck is angry with them. Friends , research shows that the comfort zone is really a trap ! It's really a dangerous place because it prevents you from improving your current state and gives you the feeling that everything is hunky dory . It makes you feel that your life was destined for it and the current situation is inescapable & best for you . It plays upon your insecurity and constant fear and makes it impossible for you to achieve all the things you are capable of achieving . Let me share with you a short story . This is the everyday routine of Mr Ravi , a young sales professional from Gurgaon for the last 10 years . He gets up angry in the morning and reluctantly goes to the office because he hates his boss & his boss equally hates him. Ravi knows that his salary is less than the competition but still he remains stuck due to insecurity of job . He is seen always complaining that his life is very monotonous , like a rat in a hamster wheel . Every day he follows the same routine and comes back home sad , miserable and dejected . Do you know what is that one thing that is stopping him from growing higher and setting him apart from the crowd? Is this your story or someone known to you ? Well , it is his inability to come out of his comfort zone and the sad part is that this is not just the story of Ravi but several million human beings across the globe as most of them compromise or adjust to be in their current situations and decide to remain stuck forever . So , like a hamster wheel , they just keep on running but the truth is that they will never reach any destination because day after day while the wheel keeps spinning but all remain in a stationary position. . . History shows that fortune favors only the brave . People who are courageous enough to take the leap of faith. So whether it's Thomas Edison who failed multiple times till he achieved success or Sachin Tendulkar that kept on pursuing his passion till he achieved his highest professional goals . I gave just these two names but there are several examples like Nelson Mandela , Martin King Luther , Jeff Bezos , Steve Jobs, Brian Acton and the list is endless . They all took initiatives to change themselves and the society for a better future . The important thing to remember is that we get to live once and we should never live a life of regret . Once the time passes , we all become helpless because it's non refundable . So to achieve growth in life and live a life of abundance , you need to become braver & get outside your comfort zone . Just have a conversation with your inner heart on your life goals and values ! You need to redefine all the strategies for navigating life challenges successfully under pressure . You need to break all the chains that are stopping you from handling difficult or unexpected situations. I strongly encourage all the readers of my book to make a decision today so as to change something in your life that you are unhappy with and just start experiencing positive changes. Just take one action and life will slowly take you out of your discomforts . The best way is to challenge yourself to a more difficult scenario , accept more risks, lean into desired suffering, just get comfortable with being uncomfortable. Friends , these are not plain words that I am expressing but it's the reality of life that even I have myself gone over a period of time . Initially everything will look very uncomfortable but let me assure you that this is the only way to progress and a way to achieve your unfulfilled desires. So ,whether you are an individual or an organization or a brand , all need to change their current state to move on to a higher level . Maybe it's real or maybe it is artificial , but the whole idea is to change the status quo . Acquire more knowledge , more wisdom & spend your energies so as to come out of your comfort zone. Here are my suggested three ways that can help you break the "hamster wheel": 1. Sic Parvis Magna : The motto originates back to 1587 by Sir Francis Drake's words: "There must be a beginning to any great matter, but the continuing unto the end until it be thoroughly finished yields the true glory". This means not only is the end goal important but what is necessary is to start the journey , with a small step . Because not only the end , but the journey is important which will eventually take you out from the comfort zone to the desired goal . It is a true fact that greatness comes from small steps in life . 2. Exitus acta probat: Even if you have to take some out of course actions , some unconventional moves , I suggest you should take it so that your ultimate goal is achieved . For example , let's say you want to go for higher education but your exit from the company may cause you or the company a huge financial loss ,but I suggest you still should go ahead to meet the end result of pursuing higher education .Means should justify the end ! 3. Festina Lente —It means Hurry slowly. The whole idea here is to start slowly so that it can be done in a proper way instead of rushing to any task . In order to prove someone our ourselves , we try to do things very fast or start doing multi-tasking. Sometimes it happens that we do grave mistake in the process and all efforts get wasted . I strongly suggest avoiding multitasking or doing too many things at a time . More important is to get into action , maybe do it slowly but in a proper way . Let me assure you that once you follow the above suggested three pieces of advice , it will certainly help you to come out of your comfort zone and move towards greater success . The whole difference between a thinker and doer is that action seekers just get into action .This ultimately differentiates winners from the crowd . Just as a Lotus flower stands out in the mud . Mantra is to break out of the comfort zone , live in the moment and grasp the opportunity thrown at you . Friend's, we have limited time on this earth and our "Return ticket " is confirmed ! So leave the comfort zone & challenge the status quo by thinking outside the box. Your dream is not just a dream , it's an opportunity to prove yourself and achieve your full potential .Just act now ! Tomorrow may be too late !

Alexandria Evelyn Johnson.

Alexandria Evelyn Johnson descends from The Bahamas. She is a Clinical Psychologist, Life Coach, Child Forensic Expert, and an Educator. She is also an ordained Youth Pastor and a Minister. She is the author of three children's books. She enjoys writing and going to the beach.

ZARLISH WAHID

THE TEARS THAT I HAVE CRIED ARE WET BUT DRY.

When I am alone,
I cry, cry, cry.
I cry so that I can speak
I want to be heard
Without even uttering one word

Don't cry aloud for all to hear or see.
Instead, I allow my soul to do it for me.
Dark tears fall from its face.
Overwhelming it
Devouring its space

Eyes of love are tracking my every movement
I am suffocating
I can't breathe for a moment
Don't cry aloud for all to hear or see.
Instead, I allow my soul to do it for me.
Dark tears fall from its face.
Overwhelming it
Devouring its space

Deep into
My abyss I go
To cry alone
Far away
So, no one knows

Don't cry aloud for all to hear or see.
Instead, I allow my soul to do it for me.
Dark tears fall from its face.
Overwhelming it
Devouring its space.

What a state?
This is my fate!
I can't fight it
I must obey
The urge to hide
The urge cry
It's too strong
Why strive?
When everything is wrong.

Don't cry aloud for all to hear or see.
Instead, I allow my soul to do it for me.
Dark tears fall from its face.
Overwhelming it
Devouring its space.

I once was a fighter
I once cared
I once dreamt big dreams
I once dared
To be great to be a superstar
To rule the world
Live a life of luxury
Drive fancy cars

Don't cry aloud for all to hear or see.

Instead, I allow my soul to do it for me.
Dark tears fall from its face.
Overwhelming it
Devouring its space.

Have you ever climbed a mountain?
Just to fall to the ground.
Gazing around
Ashamed
Embarrassed
Low
Chained in confounds
Trapped in a comfort zone.

Wait
I am thinking for a moment
Without fear
Without shame
Without fatigue
Without blame
Wow! I remember this claim

'For I know the plans I have for you," declares the LORD, "plans to prosper you and not to harm you, plans to give you hope and a future" (Jeremiah 29:11 NIV). The Almighty God created the universe in six days and all of its contents but etched you and me on His mind. God thinks about us through the lens of purpose. God understands fully the depth of our design and the time it took to create each of us to perfection. From this stance, He tells us that we were not here by chance, but our existence is a part of a divine plan. We were not meant just to exist, but our time spent on earth must consist of us seeking God who has plans for our lives.

We must earnestly strive to understand the purpose of our existence and activate each plan. We have a blessed assurance that the plans that God has for us will not cause us harm but will cause us to prosper. These plans are filled with hope. We have a blessed assurance that our success, and our future is secured in God.

Wow! What a day that would be
To let myself be
To grab some hope
To set me free
Reality check
I am not sure.
Sounds good.
Maybe.

Should I permit myself to be trapped in my comfort zone? If, I permit myself to be trapped in my comfort zone, then what happens to the plans that God has just for me. I am trapped in my comfort zone snuggled beside defeat. Comfort is a plushtrap. Comfort is loaded with perks. It presents no incentive to try. No pressure to give an effort. It presents a highly controlled existence where fear is the ultimate excuse to remain static. Isn't fear a good enough excuse though?

Blah! Blah! Blah!
Don't look at me with disdain
Like I am scum
You don't know my story
The times I have tried
The times I have succumbed
Rolling in defeat

While standing on my feet
Praying hard Praying to God

Have I not commanded you? Be strong and courageous. Do not be afraid; do not be discouraged, for the LORD your God will be with you wherever you go." (Joshua 1:9 NIV). We have not been promised that life would be easy. We have been commanded to be strong and courageous as we stand against life and its rolling adversities. At each moment, we have been commanded to liberate ourselves from the chains of comfort, pick ourselves up and fight. We have been promised the companionship of God even when we face our lives' most violent wars.

Are you trapped in your comfort zone?
Are you living your life by God's design?
Are you at the in-between in life?
Are you living a lie?
You decide
How you live
What will be said of you when you die.

Karthikeya.

Karthikeya was born in the month of the rainy season. As a child, he used to spend his time watching anime. He is the greatest fan of Harry Potter films and books in secret. Also, he used to spend his time crafting, writing stories, and converting episodes of anime into stories. He is a dreamy child who lives in his creative world of art and stories. His works deal with both creative and real-life events. His past work includes a short story SHOWER-it's hard to know, as a co-author in the book BLOSSOMS by Alvira publishing.

Z CELLS- SHAPE MAKERS
OF UNIVERSE

Project Z cells were first time brought to the field of science on Oct 26 in 3060 by Richard Wells, while the discussion is going on creating new species on kepler8. After which the meeting called off. "See now who is giving ideas?" Said Adam. The man who can't wear his tie properly. I don't want to say this but who cares that he solved the errors in rocket take off, no one cares. I know that. See man for decades, we are creating new species and I think Z cells could be the new phase of life on a new planet. Said, Richard. Wait man are you trying to convince me, god I have work to do if you don't mind. Said Adam. This is insane, we are living in 30th century using the energy of the sun replacing it with burning coal on earth. And still, the mind of humans has not changed a bit. SPEAKERPHONE: Emergency, code red, CO_2 is increasing in the atmosphere with 40KM/HR with time interval of 10 sec. Adam: Alert, alert. This is to say all the citizens settle in your nearby hiding indoors until the storm calms down. Richard: No, we don't have much time. I was about to reveal this a long ago but I think it's time. Our lab is connected with every house on this planet with pipes. And here is my idea, this time co2 content is higher which makes problem in breathing. So, if we can release one of the oxygen tank and supply to the houses citizens can be saved to a level of 50%. Board members: yeah, this sounds good, but the other tank is not yet ready and we can't take risk of our lives. Adam: it takes 2weeks to prepare oxygen tanks and with our new project oxy-w we can make as many as tanks within 2 days. So, let's do it. With the spot decision they took, we were able to save 70% of the population. Richard, Adam toast to you guys for taking responsibility for the lives says, board members. And "Adam right now the atmosphere, resources on the earth are polluted to a saturated level. With this it's impossible to make oxygen within 2weeks or 2days even with the project oxy-w it takes time", said Richard. Not long right, however, we are facing the storm once in 6months. So, there are possibilities we can fill up half of the tank. By the way Richard, I have asked the X-27 about Z cells. Which turns out interesting. But, as you know we are dealing with the conditions on our planet it seems a tough task. However, we can still work on it. Lights flashing: X-27 speaking, Z cells are bilateral species that are estimated to have a life span of nearly 2months, and these are seen rarely due to the atomic blast and when creatures are exposed to excessive radiation.

* * *

X-27 can you play the voice notes of Adam and Richard-asked Adell. Controlled voice: yes, here it goes. Adam speaking: It has been 42 days since the project Z cells are on the cards, after the gigantic co2 storm for the second time earth was left with countable human life. This is where we started discussing the Z cells which can survive in the extreme radar environment. Look, Dad, can we go to mars? People were saying it has a better chance of habitation than earth. Then also reminded that every month people are evacuating from earth to mars. Dad, if you hear this voice note let us know. "Richard, what are you thinking?" asked Adam. It has been 100 years since we started extracting energy from the sun and using it as a power source leaving coal to the ground. "The energy from the sun is our life source" "Don't you think it will last till generations?" "What the hell? I never said it like that" Based on our planet's situation there will be another gigantic storm in the next coming days. Which makes it hard for the living organisms to live on. So, it's time we leave for mars. Day 48: Richard speaking: Today Z cells started breaking out but few of them were so weak. THE NEXT LIGHT IS ON MARS: X-27 speaking: warning, warning, there is an underground wave evolving. Its coordinates are surpassing the surface of a planet. Evacuate, evacuate. People of planet earth speaking, we are sending you a few samples of project Z cells with a humanoid robot Z-67. Which will give you details of the project Z cells. This is Z-67 reaching the mars planet, asking you for the coordinates to land. At the point where the mars witnessed the last light of the earth.

* * *

X-28 speaking: Hello, I am A.I. of mars. Let me tour you of our planet. This is the cell where we make food for the entire planet. Every house in here is under surveillance and this is not to spy but for the safety of the planet. And now let me take you to machines from the earth, here we are. This is the curiosity rover, which is still under work. Here, from this scope, you can observe the Mars one satellite sending us information about the earth every week. Z-67 let's knock it off, now take me to the research department. "Bringing in Z-67" transferred information from the lab by X-28. These are Z cells samples, age 80 days, and can see with their eyes. "The new generation is right," says Adell. "For reference can I get the life span data of previous samplings?" "Sure, here you go?" "Results seem to be promising" "X-28 can I know? What are the things and inventions the humans have done during past decades" exclaimed Z-67. "Hopefully there is a thoughtful being I can talk to", said Z-28 "Humans started building basic needs for a living" "But, however this is not earth. Right?" "So, machines began monitoring human work" "Over the days they started constructing space stations and planning to make factories" "Never to say crazy but it is what humans are?" Emergency, storm alert: evacuate, evacuate. "X-28 we have to alert the people I heard a call evacuate" No need to worry, this voice is from the video game the kids play here named "THE EXTINCT PLANET-BLUE". "Let's call it a day A.I", said Z-67 while entering into the charging void. Jared, Marie, James, Julie I and II mom, dad look like they are showing earth on live visible. It seems like there are no people on the planet. Do you know the earth is the planet from which people came to this planet? Said James. "It was a planet with huge stars and wise people" "Dad does this mean our planet will also be in such chaos as planet earth?" asked Julie I. "There is a saying every living planet should face the dark in a few light years," said James. It's already night, move to your bed shouted Marie. Maybe new species can change the way of life in the coming million years. Answers the visiplate screen for the press questions.

* * *

Planet kepler8 A.I. speaking: Do you think there is a possibility of Z cells changing the way of life? X-28: It's a hypothetical concept. Which doesn't follow the laws of nature. To the point of research, Z-cells are a mistake and fusion of two opposite beings. "Can you even imagine a species like that?" "Truly humans are the weird inventors in the biological and galactic world" "But, maybe there is a chance that these Z-cells can help in building a world of cells, which cares about their own planet," says Kepler8 A.I. "Yeah maybe there is a possibility, let'Z-67" exclaims X-28. Slowly changing the way of sentence, Z-67 do you think that Z-cells are taking over humans? Z-67 replies, maybe we can find an answer in the next coming decades. And by the way, X-28 do you have any recordings from the earth? "Yeah, hopefully there are very few" "Here the 1st goes' ' Day 50: I suppose Dr. /you ever listen to this. Remember from day 50-60 these species vessels should be immersed in the chemical environment, electric void, and exposed natural sun for their nutrition. Kepler8 A.I. What are these species? X-28: Weird species from weird facts and experiments. Z-67: Okay guys, try to keep a low profile. We are also created from those weird sciences, don't you forget. Adele speaking: I think it's time to prepare the space shuttle to send these species to planet kepler8. "Is it possible they are 50 days old?" says X-28. "Yes, I know that but these species are about to break," said Adell "Which means the data we received is incomplete" "And we have sent these species right now" shouted Adell. Listening to its inventor, X-28 launched the mission successfully.

* * *

X-30 speaking: man considered himself a creative being. Chasing time and space to master the subject called creation. He travels to stars, galaxies and even sent his creations to space to collect the samples from the stars and to examine them to prove there is life on this star, which could be our new home. He tried new things, new species and the weird mission Z cells. After the landing Z-cells started building the oxygen banks, forests, houses, etc. every Z cell life was just for 48 days. And plants started growing from their shells, this is what the Z-cells are made to survive in the extreme radiation condition and build a life on planets. So, the task for humans becomes easy for traveling from planet to planet in the extreme conditions they make themselves to live in. Kepler8 A.I. X-30 is there a chance the Z-cells can take over on humans? "This has to be answered by Z-67" Z-67: I can say it's time, you have to search for the unheard recordings X-30. X-30: These are the last two recordings I saved. RICHARD SPEAKING: On the 230th day, Z-cells will travel through space reaching stars and create life on planets. And for every million to Trillion years these Z-cells break out on the stars to keep the planet's shape in a natural cycle. And Z-cells are the species with the human form known as, "SHAPE MAKERS OF UNIVERSE". These are born with photosynthesis pores and reproducing quality, and the reproduction of the particular plant or animal takes place based on the surrounding chemical conditions. Which is why? These can reproduce new Z-cells or create a new life after extinction. "Z-cells are truly a way of new generation constructing and preserving the planet's surface for future life," says Adell. X-30:

Now, what Z-67? "Keeping nature in its very own shape and protecting the galaxy, moreover protecting our red planet from humans. I even heard from Adam saying that when you reach mars you will see children purchasing the toy models of curiosity rover and space shuttle" said Z-67. X-30: Yes, children do. But how does he even know? "I asked the same question several times" "Do you know what he said?" "Then play the last recording," said Z-67. ADAM SPEAKING:

"It is, who are we? Humans."

Mujahid Iqbal.

Having academically honored from renowned central university AMU during 2001. Handful of paper says undersigned nurtured electrically into engineering recipe and embedded with no title of its own almost half of the life spent serving corporate organization in management role . Out of 20 odd years, he spent 6 good years in India and remaining in UAE ���� Oman ���� Qatar ���� & Finland ����. Worked with Bihar State Electricity Board In year 2006 as JE Town , fortunately got courage to put an end on bribe system & left within 6 month of joining due to " Old Habit Die Hard " nature. Year 2019 August put undersigned on stake and career journey didn't progress further connection to the other world and pushed him away to stay in the motherland. Keeping high hope with ability to fight back and started a new JOB with GE as a PM. Quite long but not more than a baby birth calendar the deadly virus �� poured toxic recipe in atmosphere keeping everyone shocked & Shattered. " A Race in Career " became Hide n Seek game of childhood memories & finally August 2020 battle of career journey again lost . Quite a long but it's never too late to start , hope & struggle gave undersigned enough strength to move on with textiles business due to pandemic. Year 2021 February Undersigned became an entrepreneur in textiles industry and since then serving society that makes people unique in their outfit. Loneliness is not in his dictionary though Undersigned always engage himself in extracurricular activities like Paper Calligraphy art , Architectural Model making , exploring innovative ideas, love to write couplets " Shayari" running a FB page by name " Naghma-e-Zindagi" where you can find 100s of his lovely couplets. Not all alone fortunately undersigned have passion towards delicacies and continental recipes unfortunately one can't have same pinch on second invitation����. Haven't heard of rainbow �� Biryani fortunately He dared to try differently.�� Undersigned is straight on talk with great patience and an Ardent learner hope and patience is his best friend though. Regards ,

Mujahid Iqbal Reach me @7870637076 (WhatsApp) Email:- mujahidleo@gmail.com

IG:- mujahidleoinsta , naghmaezindagi

A pleasant morning always reminds of the new beginning of life taking place soon no matter how hard time spent from dawn to dusk. It is always good to experience the variety of waves passing through the phases of life. This one that can be overlooked and keep moving while the other which makes you adjustable to that vary cause. Comfortable is not just getting ready for bed, rather it's a state of mind that creates a balanced synergy of mental peace , soulful emotions and muscular stress. The overall quality of comfort is the state of mental peace and adaptive nature who retrospect irrespective of the situation. Patience is worth admiring when you eventually overcome that sets to happen all through the time. Nevertheless, the vary cause is not that important but how to handle such a situation is of big concern yet many of us fail to understand and cope up with. Subsequently engulfed in various pre and post metal stresses raising questions on self-conscience and mental strength. Somehow, every one of us is found trapped by such phenomenon where comfort is being questioned now and then. To define comfort is in general understanding a state of commitment that fulfill the requirements and there's no question later on to ponder upon. Likewise sky and land never meets at any point of time , need of human can't be met in totality but yes when Contentment is done comfort is achieved. Trapped in comfort zone often open the doors to pros and cons. Let us take an example of trapping in comfort for a longer period of time from the very early stage of life say childhood. The climatic temperature is favorable to your body by adjusting a balance temperaments for couple of years unfortunately if somehow changed it's difficult rather impossible to return to state of mind which created a comfortable balance. Always time is best healer but it needs stretch of patience and a good amount of strength to help you keep calm and get adjusted to the change. Life teach us variety of situations from cradle to grave and one needs to be patient with strength to handle and cope up to go farther in journey of happiness. Trapping and engulfing within comfort zone is quite phenomenal however we should always try to return in our original form. We should build our survival is the fittest theory enough to keep calm and supportive in situations where many of us fail to understand just because of impatience. Life is a journey between cradle to grave hence there's nothing doubtful about life rather one should be very diligent and ardent in learning to survive. " The one who is down needs fear not fall" is quite a motivational as well as inspirational statement by the great William Wordsworth that truly depicts our style of acceptance during the journey of life. You should be more worth when your steps are on the soil and you understand the pain of others. Somehow everyone of us is trapped in our comfort zone irrespective of progressive nature in fact metaphorical behavior. Although the anonymous statement " No gain without Pain" is too irritating but makes a clear sense of understanding yet many of us lack visionary guidance towards such situations.

Michael Okami.

Started his writing Journey on Wattpad and switched to Instagram, where he publishes short poems from time to time.

T wo Hearts Apart Three Years passed by...
Peace and Freedom all over the Realms

Everyone is Happy though...

(King of the desert approached, while his daughter upfront)

Luisa are you still sulking around?

Yeah...

Is it him again,

who you think about?

But aren't you happy in your present relationship?

I really had no doubt.

Of all the men I loved,

he was the most precious one.

He was so real! Charming! Amused me all the time!

And now the one I'm in love with is just another man

who can't really show his feelings while on the other hand He:

Oh Leonardo! *crying and sobbing

He showed me all his passionate feelings.

Whence we were together I felt like the time stopped

or a million hours passed by without knowing, while we

were just looking at each other.

And, no one could ever be better than him.

Stop! Luisa please, the father I am,

I dare You! It is his own fault

he switched place with you

so we could live our life

while he's now imprisoned by this

unholy curse of a demon lord.

We're more than save here now,

He gifted us with our freedom!

He's our savior indeed!

Indeed! Oh what a blasphemy!

Even for me It pains in my own heart

what torture he must go through.

I'm really sad too..

It is so unfair!

Is the Possible really that Unpossible?

Oh what a tragedy it was!

(The Overseer stepped in the room.)

Oh me Lady, Luisa! Princess! It's Time! It's Time!

I kept this a Secret to all of you! Me, the Overseer,

who knows far more than all of you!

You Luisa, oh greatest of all the princess,

magical talent within you, through and through!

Only you have the might to save him!

As Father I forbid you to speak such unholy untruths!

How is that possible? The evil realm is far mightier

than even our own Kingdom? Speak Up!

As You can see, Princess,

The Truth is that you love the Imprisoned!

And that's where you will find your win!

I hereby summon a Portal!

Shalt Thou go through!

Thy Love Awaits You!

But wait, wait!

Can I lift the curse that's within Him?

If I free Leonardo and claim him back!

Will there be no attack?

(The one who hid himself behind the door came out of his hideout.)

Make Thyself no worries!

I Diego, your hopeless Love, will support Thee!

No matter the outcome.

We're Ready, because I made an Allegiance

Other friendly realms will help thee.

After all three new years are gone!

Have you been here all the Time!

Oh Diego! Forgive me!

Don't be!

I knew there was something strange

between you and me.

Even when I never showed

how great my Love really was,

my adoration there in Plenty.

I'm bowing deeply.

Now, now!

Stop with all the flattery!

I, the Overseer, beg my pardons.

Through the Portal thou shalt Go!

Princess remembered what I said.

The Fire within will Burn

The frozen curse

(Luisa went through the Portal)

Sensation of cold

Nowhere found

A magical sphere?

Blending the frozen threat

To make myself a crystal

Like Everyone around

Questioning myself where thou are

Though in this frozen Palace

I feel this familiar feeling

Stronger and Stronger

My heart's pounding

Wants to see thyself again

Then all of a sudden

I found thy crystalized

By all the cold And all because of me

I will never leave you behind

You're one of a kind

And I was so blind

So hesitant in that time

I will cherish you every minute

What do I have to offer to free you

(Droplet of Tears came from The Princess eyes and felt upon the crystal)

As the man came back alive

So went the darkness and pain

In this frozen Palace away

Started to feel the warmth

Light went on

Our love Proven

By a passionately long

Hug

Our Bond Forever!

That's what Love makes us!

Whence You made the Step!

Together We will be!

Without any: Regret!

The End…

So get out of your comfort zone. Because then you will make so many discoveries you wouldn't have had when you just stayed in this comfy area. Like in your bed. Oh what a threat. (giggling)

Dr. P. Gandhimathi

She's a Professor,poet , Motivational speaker and social Activist. She has published many books in Tamil(Available in Amazon Kindle) pen name : Unmathi

Qualification: B.Sc, B.Ed,M.Sc, M.Phil, M.A (cs), Ph.D

Designation : Professor Publications; More than six Book (including Education based , General books and one autobiography) Nativity : Tirupur, Tamilnadu

"ZONE OF LIFE"

Ohh !!
Our friendship is not yet strong

Enough to share the ups and downs!

She is so sweet to travel with

But

Not as easy as everyone else!

You have to study the past and the future

to understand her!

Somebody will come and go quickly

without leaving a trace!

But she is exceptional!

I have not completed any single seconds

after meeting her.

I have never walked the trail on any

given day without following in the footsteps of

nature!

Behold, I stand on the sore of the river,

Soaked with the warmth of her love!

Like everyone else I can't say that

She is the cornerstone of friendship!

Because,

Not all the friendship are the same,

Her love is greater than the value of the total wealth in

the world!

I'm proud of earning everything overall!

Everyone who is acquainted with me,

Including her also said that the intensity of love will

decrease as the days go by!

As the days go by the nail of the tree will penetrate and

how the depth of your love will diminish and disappear?

Yes , the name I pronounce more and more

Every day is your name next to God's name!

I don't know

If you've been in my memory so closely,

Even if it's probably been like you!

There is no time and no distance for your love

You are the one who is with me forever!

The friendship we've lost within ourselves does not make

me lonely

except to become a day-to-day novelty!

A thought in my soul because something has been

accomplished.

I knew in that look that you love me and that I love you!

The period of our friendship that will continue

even if you move in my opposite direction!

You think of me every seconds

I know ,

Because I'm just breathing !

How can you alone forgive and acknowledge our

a mistake?

Aree

Areeb
has al
reach
comp
where
writes

The reason is that

our ancestors have damaged you as much as possible

and we too!

Only because of the mother's heart can you forgive us.

We will not destroy you anymore

And

We will not destroy your baby in the womb!

It's easy to earn what is not in the world

But

It's rare not to destroy what is!

Thank you for forgiving our mistake!!!

We will take your love and value to our next generation.

Yes,

We will trapped our children with your comfort zone

The reason is your love is unconditional.

Our friendship is strong enough today to share our up

and downs!

Z

D

D

B